Driving Along
ROUTE
66

Amanda Jackson Green

Consultant

Brian Allman
Principal
Upshur County Schools, West Virginia

Publishing Credits

Rachelle Cracchiolo, M.S.Ed., *Publisher*
Emily R. Smith, M.A.Ed., *SVP of Content Development*
Véronique Bos, *VP of Creative*
Dona Herweck Rice, *Senior Content Manager*
Dani Neiley, *Editor*
Fabiola Sepulveda, *Series Graphic Designer*

Image Credits: p7 Alamy Stock Photo/Science History Images; p9 Library of Congress [LC-USZ62-56051]; p11 (top) Library of Congress [https://chroniclingamerica.loc. gov/lccn/sn83045462/1951-06-10/ed-1/seq-126/]; p11 (bottom) Library of Congress [LC-DIG-highsm-49556]; p12 Getty Images/Kurt Hutton; p13 (top) Library of Congress [LC-DIG-mrg-01504]; p14 Library of Congress [https://chroniclingamerica.loc.gov/lccn/ sn83045499/1928-06-08/ed-1/seq-1/]; p16 Shutterstock/Eddie J. Rodriquez; p17 (top) Shutterstock/DCA88; p17 (bottom) Library of Congress [LC-DIG-highsm-04004]; p18 Shutterstock/StockPhotoAstur; p19 Shutterstock/Nagel Photography; p20 Alamy Stock Photo/Cavan Images; p21 (bottom) Shutterstock/Moab Republic; p22 Library of Congress [HAER CAL,48-VALL,1--118]; p25 Shutterstock/Ehrlif; p27 Library of Congress [https:// chroniclingamerica.loc.gov/lccn/sn83045462/1951-06-10/ed-1/seq-126/>]; all other images from iStock and/or Shutterstock

Library of Congress Cataloging-in-Publication Data

Names: Green, Amanda Jackson, 1988- author.
Title: Driving along Route 66 / Amanda Jackson Green.
Description: Huntington Beach, CA : TCM, Teacher Created Materials, [2023] | Includes index. | Audience: Grades 4-6 | Summary: "Route 66 is one of America's most famous roads. For more than 60 years, the highway carried travelers from east to west. The route inspired inventions and created many unique jobs. It also captured the love of thousands of road trippers"-- Provided by publisher.
Identifiers: LCCN 2022021283 (print) | LCCN 2022021284 (ebook) | ISBN 9781087691084 (paperback) | ISBN 9781087691244 (ebook)
Subjects: LCSH: United States Highway 66--History--Juvenile literature. | Automobile travel--United States--History--20th century--Juvenile literature.
Classification: LCC HE356.U55 G64 2023 (print) | LCC HE356.U55 (ebook) | DDC 388.10973--dc23/eng/20220603
LC record available at https://lccn.loc.gov/2022021283
LC ebook record available at https://lccn.loc.gov/2022021284

Shown on the cover is Route 66.

Teacher Created Materials

5482 Argosy Avenue
Huntington Beach, CA 92649
www.tcmpub.com

ISBN 978-1-0876-9108-4

Table of Contents

One Road, Many Journeys

Route 66 is one of America's most famous roads. It is also called the Main Street of America or the Mother Road. The two-lane street was among the first major U.S. highways. It once stretched more than 2,000 miles (3,200 kilometers). At the start of the route was the windy, chilly city of Chicago, Illinois. Travelers who followed the path to the finish line landed in bright, sunny Santa Monica, California. Along the way, drivers explored grassy plains, dry deserts, and other amazing views.

In many ways, Route 66 changed American life. From farmers to movie stars, millions of people from all over the world drove its length. Along the way, trade expanded and new forms of **commerce** soared. Families moved from east to west and back again. Businesses sprouted up to serve tired and hungry travelers. Small, sleepy towns turned into trendy places to visit. The journey became as special as the destination. Route 66 road trips inspired songs, books, and TV shows. The road in its original form existed for just 60 years. But it lives on in the hearts of travelers to this day.

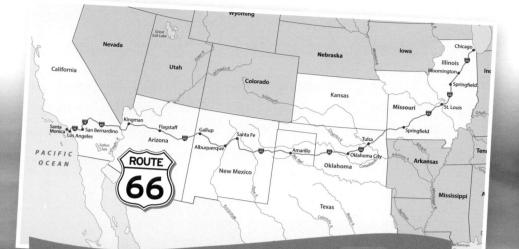

Interstate Travel

Historic Route 66 crossed eight states: Illinois, Missouri, Kansas, Oklahoma, Texas, New Mexico, Arizona, and California. Kansas had the shortest section at just 13 miles (21 kilometers). Covering 487 miles (784 kilometers), the longest stretch was in New Mexico.

Paving a New Path

The story of Route 66 begins in 1908. That year, Henry Ford invented a new kind of car. He called it the Model T. It was not the first automobile in America. But past versions were very costly. Few people could afford to own a car. Most families got around by foot, horseback, or carriage.

Ford's car cost $850 in 1908, but over time that lowered to less than $300. The lower price gave more people a chance to buy one. Car sales grew quickly. By 1924, ten million cars had been made. But this new form of travel remained a challenge. Poor roads made driving unsafe. Few roads existed to connect towns and cities.

cars and carriages on
New York's 5th Avenue, 1900

John Woodruff and Cyrus Avery came up with a plan to improve car travel. The businessmen proposed a new route. The first part of the road would go through Illinois, Missouri, Kansas, and Oklahoma. It would continue west through Texas, New Mexico, Arizona, and California. Woodruff and Avery thought the plan would increase jobs in towns along the road.

The plan was approved by the Bureau of Public Roads on November 11, 1926. Workers soon began to build Route 66.

Assembly Lines

Henry Ford's factories were the first to use **assembly lines** to build cars. Parts moved along a conveyor belt. Workers lined up along the belt, and each completed one step in putting the cars together. The process allowed Ford to produce more cars in less time.

It took workers over a decade to finish paving Route 66. Road signage went up in 1927, about a year after the road plan was approved. But state leaders oversaw building the road in each area, and crews moved at different speeds. The project was finally completed in 1938.

At first, the road was traveled mainly by farmers. They drove from their fields to city markets. There, they sold fruits, vegetables, and other goods.

In the 1930s, a severe **drought** hit the Great Plains region. Poor farming practices and little rainfall led crops to fail. From Texas to Nebraska, people died from a lack of food and water. Harsh windstorms filled the sky with black and red dust. This earned the region the nickname the "Dust Bowl." In the coming years, nearly 2.5 million people fled the area. They headed west along Route 66 in search of a better life. Many settled in California, where the soil was ripe for planting.

In 1941, the United States entered World War II. Route 66 saw a major rise in traffic at this time. The military used the road to transport troops and supplies across the country. Others made the trek west on the road, seeking jobs in wartime factories.

buried farm machinery during the time of the Dust Bowl, 1936

A family escapes the Dust Bowl in their car in 1935.

The Mother Road

Author John Steinbeck was the first person to refer to Route 66 as the Mother Road. The nickname appeared in his book, *The Grapes of Wrath*. The novel tells the story of a family traveling west in search of work during the Dust Bowl.

New Way to Vacation

World War II ended in 1945. Soon, the U.S. **economy** began to bounce back. The G.I. Bill of Rights was passed. This law gave certain benefits to former soldiers. It included money to pay for college, homes, and farms. Factories no longer needed to make weapons. Instead, companies hired people to build **consumer goods**. Workers produced goods such as cars, furniture, and appliances. Many Americans had more money than before the war. They also had more free time to spend their earnings.

By 1955, more than 52 million Americans owned a car. This new way to travel led to a popular pastime: the road trip. Families, young couples, and friends flocked to Route 66. Some stopped to enjoy national parks or visit loved ones. Others made the trek to places like the new Disneyland theme park.

This filling station on old Route 66 is on the National Register of Historic Places.

An Economic Boom

Drivers on Route 66 needed places to get their cars fixed or fill their gas tanks. They had to rest their heads after a long day's journey, too. In small towns along the route, residents started new businesses to meet these demands. Filling stations, repair shops, motels, and souvenir shops served tourists and created jobs for locals.

What's in a Name?

The word *motel* was first used in 1925. It is a combination of two common words: *motor* and *hotel*. With bigger parking lots and rooms with easy outdoor access, motels were created to meet the needs of road travelers.

Hot Food, Fast

Road trips also changed the way Americans eat. Travelers wanted fresh meals on the go. Restaurants had to find ways to serve hot food quickly. Fast food became more and more popular. Famous burger stands, such as McDonald's and Jack in the Box, were founded in the 1950s. Instead of plates, these eateries served food in paper bags and wrappers. This made it easy for customers to eat in their cars and get back on the road.

The first drive-through window opened in 1947 in Springfield, Missouri. Diners at Red's Giant Hamburg ordered and picked up their food without leaving their cars. This new invention made roadside dining even faster. Travelers wanted this quick service when they returned home, too. Fast food joints started to pop up in big cities and small towns alike.

The new food service **industry** created more jobs. Restaurants often gave jobs to teens and college students looking for short-term work. As a result, young people had more money to spend. Companies began to advertise music, movies, and clothes to this new group of consumers.

drive-through burger restaurant, 1951

early McDonald's® sign on Route 66 in California

Move Over, Dollar Menu

McDonald's® became famous for using an assembly line to get orders out quickly. The restaurant was able to sell more food in less time. This helped keep costs down. In 1954, a McDonald's burger cost just 15 cents!

Sights and Spectacles

Advertising played a big role in the success of Route 66. In 1927, Cyrus Avery formed a new group. He named it the U.S. 66 Highway Association. The association began to think about advertising and tourism. The members worked to build support for the new highway.

In 1928, the group put on a running contest. Their goal was to get people excited about Route 66. The event was called the Bunion Derby. Almost 200 athletes came from all over the world to run the race. They ran from Los Angeles to New York City. Crowds formed to cheer on the runners. Other people listened to news about the race on the radio. Famous people greeted the racers at stops along the way. The derby met its goal by bringing plenty of attention to the new highway.

ANDY PAYNE WILL LIFT MORTGAGE WITH $25,000 PYLE DERBY PRIZE

Like a true Horatio Alger hero, Andrew Pay (left), winner of the $25,000 first prize in C. C. Pyle's trans-continental marathon, will lift the mortgage on his family's Claremore, Okla., home-stead and will build a new home to replace the present cabin (above). Dad and Mother Payne (lower left); Andy's six brother and sisters, including six-year-old Will Rogers Payne (lower

A Big Finish

Andy Hartley Payne was the winner of the Bunion Derby. Payne was a runner from the Cherokee Nation. His prize was a check for $25,000. This was a huge amount of money at that time!

Route 66 also changed how businesses reached buyers. In the past, stores mostly used print advertisements. They used words and photos to sell their items in newspapers and catalogs. But shops on the Mother Road needed to attract shoppers in an instant. They used bright colors to paint their messages on billboards. Neon signs also helped attract drivers' attention.

The Bigger, the Better

By the late 1940s, commerce was booming on Route 66. Business owners competed for customers. They came up with fresh ways to lure in shoppers. These ideas ranged from fun and silly to just plain weird. Some merchants built giant statues to get attention from passing drivers. The idea was that drivers would stop to check out the statues and then buy goods from the vendor. The bigger the structure, the better!

landmark in Wilmington, Illinois

GEMINI GIANT •

One ketchup factory in Illinois built the world's largest bottle of ketchup. The bottle was 70 feet (21.3 meters) tall. Giant figures called Muffler Men popped up in front of repair shops. They portrayed ranchers, lumberjacks, and other characters. The statues got their name because they often held mufflers, which are part of an engine.

Odd museums and gift shops also convinced drivers to pull over. These places charged visitors a small fee to view strange or unusual items. Some promised views of rattlesnakes and other reptiles. Others offered tourists a chance to take home local wonders, such as shiny stones or pieces of **petrified wood**.

landmark in Holbrook, Arizona

The Blue Whale of Catoosa

One of the biggest statues still standing along historic Route 66 is a blue whale. It stands at the side of a pond in Catoosa, Oklahoma. The whale measures 80 feet (24.3 meters) long. It was a gift from a man named Hugh Davis to his wife, Zelta.

American Indians and Route 66

More than 25 American Indian tribes lived along Route 66 in its prime. About half of the route crossed tribal lands. Each tribal nation then and today has its own unique culture. The largest group is the Cherokee Nation of Oklahoma. Several Pueblo tribes live on **reservations** in New Mexico. Further west are the Navajo and Hopi peoples.

Before the Mother Road, tribal nations were quite isolated. Very few roads linked tribal lands to other parts of the country. Route 66 gave tribes more access to trade. Road travel opened new jobs for tribal members.

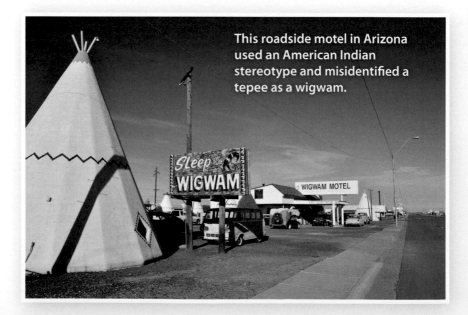

This roadside motel in Arizona used an American Indian stereotype and misidentified a tepee as a wigwam.

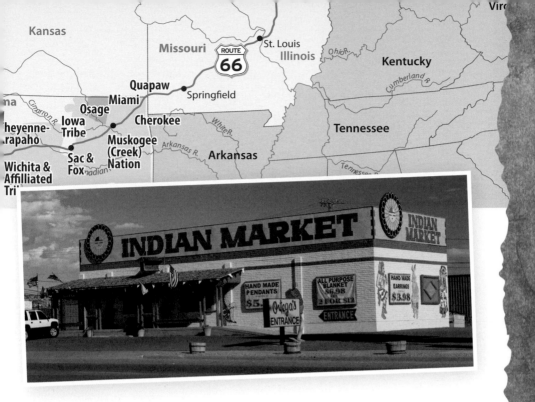

But these new opportunities did not come without harm. Many businesses used images of American Indians to draw in customers. But they based their ads on what they read in books and saw in films. Media often depicted false images of American Indians and their lives. They used **stereotypes**. Some portrayed the people as extremely violent. Other times, creators confused members of one tribe with another. For instance, one store claimed to sell Cherokee items. The store's sign showed a man wearing a war bonnet. These feathered headdresses were once common among Plains tribes. They have never been part of Cherokee culture.

American Indian Reservations

There are more than 300 reservations in the United States. Each is considered its own nation. Tribal nations must follow federal laws but not state laws. They also have their own laws, police, and courts.

Gift shops sold pipes, costumes, and other items meant to depict American Indian life. But few of these stores were owned by actual American Indians. In fact, many places on Route 66 did not allow American Indians and African Americans to enter. Some posted signs that read, "White Only."

Taking Back Tribal Images

Today, many tribes own lodges and casinos on old Route 66. These businesses provide jobs for tribal citizens. Tribes use the income to support their governments and other programs. Roadside stores sell real American Indian art. Shoppers can buy blankets, jewelry, and other crafts.

A modern Zuni artist paints a pot in a traditional style.

Some groups use tourism to teach others about their beliefs and customs. For example, the Taos Pueblo people offer village tours all year, although the COVID-19 pandemic temporarily stopped this. Others invite visitors for special holidays. On these days, tourists can witness **tribal meetings**. In these meetings, one or more tribes gather to discuss local issues. The native people also dance, sing, and make art. Sometimes, they share a feast. Each group has its own rules for visitors. Some do not allow photos. Others ask viewers to be very quiet. Following these rules shows respect for a tribe's culture.

A modern Navajo dancer does a traditional dance.

Big Money

Casinos are a major source of income for many reservations. Around 250 tribes run casinos. Visitors pay money to play betting games. Typically, American Indian casinos make more than 30 billion dollars each year.

End of the Road

By the late 1950s, most families had at least one car. Road trips remained popular. But early roads were not built for so many cars. Traffic jams were common on Route 66 and other highways. U.S. leaders needed a way to make car travel safer and quicker.

The U.S. Congress approved the Federal Aid Highway Act in 1956. The order set aside 25 billion dollars to build an **interstate system**. New roads would be wider to fit more cars. Routes also would connect to one another. This would make it easier to drive from one state to the next. New highways replaced parts of Route 66. Interstate 40 took over the longest part of the route. One end is on the East Coast in North Carolina. The other end is in California.

construction of an interstate, Vallejo, California, 1958

Even though parts of Route 66 still exist, it is no longer an official highway. In 1985, leaders decided to **decommission** Route 66. Workers removed all the road's signs. Today, about 85 percent of the historic road is open for driving. However, little funding exists to maintain it.

Drive Time

Cars were a luxury in the 1920s. Now, most American families own at least one car. U.S. drivers spend on average 17,600 minutes on the road each year! That is almost an hour every day.

Preserving America's Main Street

Drivers from all over the world still travel the historic Route 66 and visit famous stops. Tourists spend about 38 million dollars on the route each year. But new highways bypass many towns that travelers used to frequent. Locals relied on tourists for their income. With fewer customers, a lot of shops and diners had to close. **Poverty** has increased in many of these areas.

Some people are trying to revive Route 66 travel. They believe it is important to save the road's sites and history. In 1999, the National Park Service started a program to help. The group gives **grants** to companies and other groups. The money can be used to maintain buildings or do research about Route 66.

Information about Route 66 and other historic sites can be found online.

One example is in Clinton, Oklahoma. That is the home of the Route 66 Museum. The museum teaches people about the Mother Road. Visitors can check out old cars, photos, and other items. About 50,000 people visit the museum each year. That is roughly five times more than the number of people who live in Clinton!

Forest of Stones

Petrified Forest National Park is a popular Route 66 detour. Millions of years ago, trees died. Some fell into streams or were washed away by floods. They were covered with mud, sand, and volcanic ash. Over time, the logs took on these minerals and turned into stone. This led to large fields of colorful logs. Visitors can drive through the park. There are also a few spots open for hiking.

Not Quite in the Rearview Mirror

There are few roads more well-known than Route 66. The Mother Road is more than just asphalt and gravel. It is a symbol of great change. Along with the rise of cars, it shifted the course of U.S. history. The road began as a new way to get around. Over the years, it turned into a way to connect, trade, and make memories. Route 66 has served as an escape from famine and a road to victory. It means something different to each traveler who has crossed its path.

Most importantly, the Main Street of America was a link between people and places. It inspired inventions and formed brand-new areas of commerce. Road travel offered an exciting new hobby for tourists. For locals along the route, it was a new way to earn a living. In general, it transformed the ways Americans travel, eat, and market goods and services.

Even though the iconic Route 66 signs are long gone, the spirit of the road remains. Across the globe, people remain curious about its past and hopeful about its future.

The Pacific Coast Highway

Route 66 is not America's only famous road. The Pacific Coast Highway is another popular route for road trippers. About 656 miles (1,056 kilometers) long, it runs north and south along the California coast.

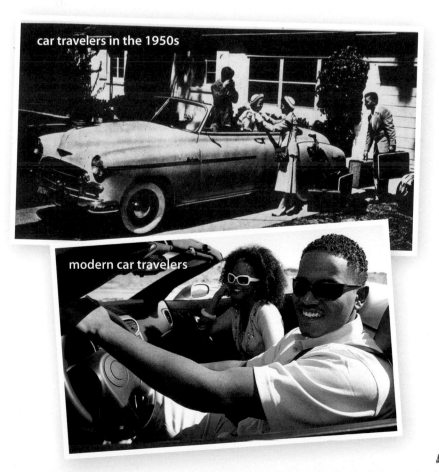

car travelers in the 1950s

modern car travelers

Map It!

Plan your own Route 66 road trip! You will make a map to help you. Follow these steps:

1. Print a map of the United States. Draw a line to show Route 66. It should begin in Santa Monica, California. It should cut straight across Arizona, New Mexico, and the Texas Panhandle. Then, it should go diagonally across Oklahoma, Kansas, Missouri, and Illinois. End it in Chicago.
2. Choose one special city or town to visit. Learn about your destination. Then, draw a symbol to mark your location on the map.
3. Choose another special city or town, and do the same for it. Do this for three or four locations. You could use a star for one city. You might mark another with a circle. Each city should have its own special mark.
4. Make a map key. On a blank sheet of paper, list the names of the cities you chose to visit. Next to the name of each city, draw the same symbol you used to mark its place.
5. Now that you know where you're going, think about your trip plans. How many days will your trip take? What will you need to pack for the journey?

Glossary

advertising—the business of making the public aware that a product or service is for sale

assembly lines—lines of machines and workers in a factory that build a product by passing work from one station to the next until the product is finished

commerce—activities that relate to the process of buying and selling goods and services

consumer goods—products that people buy for personal use or for use at home

decommission—to officially stop using something or remove something from service

drought—a long period of time when there is very little or no rain

economy—the system of making, selling, and buying goods and services in a particular place

grants—amounts of money that are given to people by a government or company to be used for a certain purpose

industry—a group of businesses that provide a particular product or service

interstate system—a network of U.S. highways that connect the 48 contiguous states

petrified wood—wood that has been turned to stone

poverty—the state of having little or no money, goods, or means of support

reservations—areas of land set aside for American Indian tribes

stereotypes—negative, harmful, or untrue beliefs about certain groups of people

tribal meetings—large gatherings planned by American Indians for socializing, dancing, singing and celebrating their culture

Index

Route 66, Arizona

Learn More!

Cyrus Avery was known as the "Father of Route 66." But who was he, really? Research this famous figure. Collect five to seven facts about Avery and his life. Here are some questions to consider:

* What was his childhood like?

* What did he do for work?

* What led Avery to come up with his plan for Route 66?

* How did Avery convince others to support his plan?